CHECO'S LAW
Four Words to Live By

DR. SERGIO ANDRÉS BELLO GUERRA

The Publishing Pad
www.thepublishingpad.com

Dedication

My dearest and beloved son,

Your life, though brief, stands as a testament to resilience, courage, and an unwavering spirit. Born into a world that often seemed indifferent to your unique needs, you faced countless challenges with a grace that surpassed your tender years. Your laughter, a distinctive and enchanting sound, resonated wherever you went, serving as a constant reminder of the joy you brought into our lives and to all those your existence touched. Even in the darkest of times, your spirit remained a beacon of hope, illuminating our path and guiding us toward a deeper understanding of love, compassion, and the true meaning of life. Though you may be gone, your memory endures—a cherished treasure that will forever shape our hearts.

For my precious daughter,

You are the light that brightens my every day, the radiant smile that lifts every cloud from my sky. Your laughter, like the sweetest melody, fills my heart with unending joy, and your presence is the constant rhythm that brings meaning to my life.

Every one of your small, thoughtful gestures brings me happiness, and the way you embrace life with such wonder makes the world feel more vibrant and alive. I adore you beyond measure, and each day with you is a gift I cherish deeply.

Your love, your kindness, and your spirit inspire me endlessly. You are my heart's greatest treasure, and for you I am forever grateful.

To the love of my life, my unwavering wife,

Your love has been the steadfast anchor that has kept me grounded through the stormiest seas of life. In every challenge, in every setback, you have been the light that illuminates my eyes, my guiding beacon, lighting the path forward when all seemed lost. Your unwavering belief in me, your constant support, and the depth of your love have been the pillars upon which our family and my dreams have been built.

Through every obstacle and fall, you have lifted me, not just with words of encouragement but with the quiet strength of your presence, reminding me that together we are unstoppable. You are not just my strength, you are my inspiration, my hope, and the reason I continue to strive for more. Every triumph I've achieved is a reflection of your faith in me.

You have filled my life with a joy that knows no bounds, a love that gives my heart its greatest peace. I am endlessly grateful to call you my partner, my confidante, and my best friend. Thank you for walking this journey with me, for believing in me when I couldn't, and for showing me, every day, what true love looks like.

Contents

Acknowledgement

I would like to thank Dr. Belio, Dr. Blanco, and all the doctors from the Hospital Infantil de México for their care and attention to my son. I also want to express my appreciation to Chisom Ezeh and The Publishing Pad team for all their help and advice in finally finishing and publishing the book.

Introduction

This book, the first in a series, is about a very special part of my son's life story. When he was born, doctors gave him only three months to live due to a syndrome that caused multiple disabilities. However, he defied all medical expectations and lived many years, always showing incredible independence and enjoying his life to the fullest.

From a very young age, he demonstrated a strength of will and a joy for life that inspired all of us who had the privilege of knowing him. He never complained about his condition; instead, he focused on making the most of every moment and finding happiness in the little things. His positive attitude and resilience are the core of the story I want to tell. I firmly believe his story will inspire and comfort many other families facing similar situations.

This book is based on four words or attitudes that we learned from observing my son's behavior during the time he lived with us. Each of these encapsulates a vital lesson and perspective that we learned from him. He faced life and its challenges with a strength and grace that we will always remember.

I believe this part of his story not only enriches the narrative but also highlights a message of hope and strength that is fundamental to the purpose of this book.

CHAPTER ONE

THE FOUNDATIONS

I asked my wife, "What could possibly be happening?"—putting words to what we both were thinking but had not wanted to say out loud, pretending that as long as we didn't speak about it, everything was fine.

We were greatly afraid because our son, Sergito, had been in the operating room for a little over two and half hours, yet nobody had come out to tell us what the doctor was doing with our son or what our little son was going through. How much more time was going to pass before someone would come out?

We were completely exasperated because we did not know anything at all.

This was not the first time Checo had been in this situation (our son Sergito went by many nicknames, including Checo). For most of his life we had been in and out of hospitals with him, sometimes getting out fairly quickly, but on other occasions, the majority, facing high chances that he was not going to make it due to the mortal characteristics of his syndrome.

Looking at the peaceful and beautiful face of my wife sent me back to the first time I saw her at the tennis club, the moment I met her, and the process of getting her to be my girlfriend and my beloved wife for all these years and for what is left of our lives.

I lived in Oaxaca, México, in the late 1970s and the 1980s. It was a completely different time as far as the way the world used to do things. People got married because they really loved each other.

The moment I had the good fortune to see this beautiful and amazing girl, I knew immediately that she was going to be the love of my whole life even though we did not meet until much later. She was playing tennis at the club—the only tennis club in my hometown at the time—and I knew, inside myself, the incredible, wonderful and marvelous human being she was. I tried to talk to her, but I was so shy and had so little self-esteem that I could not do it, and I let the opportunity slip away.

Fortunately, my friends and I had the custom of going to play tennis every weekend at the same club, and I saw her there every time. My desire to meet her grew, but so did my fear of approaching her. I wanted to ask her if we could be friends and, if things went well, for her to be my girlfriend and maybe, one day, my wife.

Time went by, and I went away from my hometown to study abroad for my junior year of high school. My feelings and thoughts for this amazing girl just went to sleep, as if forgotten and cleaned up.

However, one year later, I was back home for my last year of high school, and when I walked into the classroom for the first class of the semester, there she was! The moment I saw her, my heart just flipped 360 degrees with feelings of amazing warmth and tenderness. I decided that this time I was not going to lose her again. I was determined not to let her slip from my fingers when I had just gotten the opportunity to capture her heart.

But I still was very shy, so it took me almost three months to pluck up the courage to declare my feelings to her. When I finally found the strength to do it, I started as most of us do in this situation when we are afraid of what the woman might say: "What would you say if I asked you to be my girlfriend?"

She replied, "Are you asking me to be your girlfriend, or do you just want to know out of curiosity?" Then she smiled, a smile that melted me completely.

Feeling like a fool, I said, "No, what I mean is would you like to be my girlfriend, really." I was really embarrassed that I hadn't handled the situation better.

But she knew how to handle it, just like the queen that she is. Smiling and blushing a little, she told me to save that question until later that afternoon at the movies, where I had already invited her.

So, here I was with my heart jumping around crazily in my chest and my mind playing games with me with questions like: *Will she turn me down? Will she give me a chance? Or will she just ignore the question completely?*

After our little chat that morning at school, I could not wait to see her again, but the time went by painfully slowly. All day long, I was watching the clock and counting the minutes as they went by. My plan was to leave school immediately at the end of the day and run to meet her at her house instead of meeting her at the movies. My heart and my feelings did not want to miss one precious instant of looking at her beauty. By picking her up instead of meeting her at the movies, I could spend as much time with her as possible.

I was so nervous that, at first, I could not find the money to pay for our tickets. The lady at the ticket counter had one of those faces that all ticket sellers seem to have: serious, no smile, formal and not talkative at all, yet at that moment I thought she was smiling at me and giving me courage to go ahead and, finally, get my love's yes answer.

We got the tickets, went into the movie theater, found our seats, and sat down. We talked about nothing, just like two very nervous young people in love waiting for the right moment to make a very big decision for their future. As we waited for the movie to start, I did not dare to ask her the question she had told me to save. My heart was bumping all around in my chest, my stomach was full of butterflies, and I really did not know what to do.

I thought over and over again, *What if she really doesn't like me?*

Then: *But, no! If that would be the case, why did she agree to go with me to the movies, and why did she say she would give me an answer there?*

Again: *Maybe she just said it to be nice so I would not feel so bad, or so nobody at school would see my disappointment when she says no.*

These thoughts filled my head as I watched her beautiful smiling face. She was being amazingly nice, as always, and I acted completely calm and relaxed, totally the opposite of how I felt inside of me.

Finally, the movie started. I remember it had something to do with a motorcycle gang, but at that moment, that movie was the least important thing in my entire world. I took a very deep breath, and then, gathering all the strength I could find, which I have to say was not much, I turned my head to her and asked her: "Would you like to be my girlfriend?"

She looked at me, smiled, and gently said what would be one of the most amazing answers of my whole life, comparable only to when she agreed to be my wife. She said, "Yes! Yes, I would like to be your girlfriend."

So, I turned my head completely to her beautiful face, moved closer, and gave her my first kiss on the edge of her mouth.

I was so astonished I could not breathe. I felt like I was flying. *Yes, she told me yes, she loves me as I do her! Yes, she said yes! Now she is my girlfriend, and I will love her and keep her by my side for all our lives!*

The movie went on, of course, but for me the only thing important and alive in the whole world at that moment was her, the love that I felt for her, and my happiness at her answer. I felt that the future was going to be so brilliant with her by my side, and I really could not think of anything else.

"Relax, my love." My wife's lovely voice brought me back to the present and to what was happening in the hospital with our son. "They probably are having some problems with his esophagus. Remember that it is very difficult to do any kind of endoscopy on him due to all the operations he has already had. The doctor must be very careful to do what it takes to see why he is unable to swallow anything."

And, of course, she was right. Gastric acid reflux, one of the symptoms of our son's syndrome, had completely burned his esophagus, requiring several difficult reconstructive surgeries.

Trying to stay calm after my wife's reminder, I started to think about how our life was before we got married and had Sergito— after she gave me the *yes* that answered all my prayers, finally becoming, after all the years I had been after her, my girlfriend and, for me and my future, my wife forever.

Our life as boyfriend and girlfriend started when we were class-mates. We were in the last year of high school. She was in another classroom for the first semester, but every time we could possibly be together—between classes, anytime we had the slightest possibility—we were by each other's side. Every day I was at her house after school to be with her, talk, and, of course, do what all boyfriends and girlfriends do and have a marvelous time together.

The last semester, we were together in the same classroom and spent almost the whole day together. I went back to my house only to sleep, and then the next day we were back at school, together all the time, loving and enjoying each other.

But, as it should be, time went by, and high school ended. I had to go away from her to study for my career because her mother would not let her go away from home at the beginning, so we cried, and I departed to start building the life I wanted to have with her. I would have to be far away from her for several years until I could come back and marry her.

Or so I thought.

Six months after I went away, she called to tell me that she was going to study at the same university and campus where I was. Imagine the shock and the happiness I felt!

We were going to share our studies for the next four years in the same place, and we were going to be together and share everything from now on—except nights, when she had to go, of course, as we were not married yet and times were completely different then. She slept in the student residences, I in my rented house.

Our lives were great. Each of us was studying what we wanted. Of course, every semester she beat me in grades; even though I tried hard to outdo her, every single semester she had better grades than me. Life was amazing. I had all that I wanted at that moment, and time went by, as it should be.

Then I finished my degree and graduated. My father insisted I should get a job in what seemed to me like record time, but I did it, and I started my professional life in an exceptionally good way. I got a job in precisely the field I had studied for: software engineering. So, I was doing what I enjoyed and was very well paid at the same time. The company that hired me was great; it was international, so I had to travel to provide support to different businesses around the country. I had great benefits and time to be with my girlfriend all that time.

She kept on with her studies, and then, as time went by, she also finished her degree. She graduated, and then we had to decide what we were going to do with our lives at that moment. We wanted to be together and never have to be apart again, but there was a slight problem. It was a very hard problem at the time. Companies were not hiring. In fact, they were firing more and more people each day, mainly from the executive positions. Every single time you looked at the news, there was another closure or bankruptcy at this or that enterprise. México was in the worst economic crisis of its entire history. Inflation was incredibly high, and money in México was worth less and less with each passing day. One day you could buy something, and the next day it would cost twice as much or even more.

So, this is the time when my girlfriend got out of college. She had graduated with high honors with a degree in economics from the same university where I graduated, yet there was no way for her to get a job in her field. She would have to go back to our hometown, and then our opportunities to see each other would be very scarce, maybe once or twice a year, and we did not want that. We wanted to keep our love alive and to share everything together all the time.

Therefore, we decided, after five years and two months of engagement, to get married, to live the rest of our lives together, sharing the good and the bad, the poverty and the richness, the health and the sickness, and, mainly, to love each other as much as we did at that moment.

"Finally, there is the doctor."

The comment from my wife brought me back from my memories to the present, where we were so worried for our son. Immediately we went running to meet the doctor and hear what he had to say about the operation and how Sergito was doing.

"It is really hard to break up what he ate," the doctor started to explain. "Apparently, he swallowed a big hot dog whole. The food is so soft, it is difficult to break it up. If I push a little too hard and the endoscope moves away, it could perforate the esophagus, and then Sergio would die."

That last comment was the hardest one to hear.

The doctor continued: "I must keep on working slowly and gently, so it will take some more hours to finish. So, please be patient and wait for me to call you when we finish."

Then he turned around and returned to the operating room without letting us say the slightest word or ask him any of the thousands of questions that came to our minds.

It was the same situation as we had experienced several times during our son's life. Because of the severity of his illness, urgent operations were a normal thing in our lives, though that is not to say it was easy to stay calm. It was difficult to have to wait and hope that everything was going to be okay.

But, as the doctor walked away, my wife said to me, "Sergito is going to be fine. Remember, he is very strong and wants to keep on living and staying with us."

She seemed so convinced, as she always had in all the times of trouble, that I had to be as sure as she was that everything was going to be okay.

"I know, my love," I said. "I know that he speaks directly with God and that he decides to stay with us. I think even if God did not want him to stay, Sergito would know how to convince Him."

"Remember," my wife said, "the four words to live for that we found together with Sergito and remember all the things that our life together has taught us. When we apply those principles, we are happy, and we get what we want. Now it is time to put them to work again."

"Yes," I said, "you are right."

Then we went silent and waited for the doctor to finish the operation and for the chance to see our little son well again.

After more than another hour of waiting anxiously, my mind started to wander again.

It was May 1982 when I graduated. I had just finished my degree in computer science, and I was about to start my professional life. We were at the graduation prom when suddenly my father took me aside. With all his seriousness, he said to me: "Congratulations, son, for this great accomplishment you had already achieved. But now you will have to achieve something greater in less than thirty days."

I was completely astonished. I thought he would be incredibly happy and proud because I graduated. I did not know what he meant, so I asked: "What do you mean by that?"

"That you will have to get a job by the end of the month. I will keep on giving you your allowance until then," he clarified, "but after that day, you will have to pay for your rent, your care, and everything else by yourself."

"Are you serious?" I asked.

"You know that I am always serious about money matters."

And I knew that was completely true. If there is one thing my father never made a joke about, it was money.

So, I was devastated. Here I was, having just finished my degree, and my father dropped a bomb.

I was shocked! I could not believe what he was saying. My father was telling me that his obligations to me were over, and now it was my turn to take care of me.

Of course, I knew and completely agreed that when one has a way to work and support oneself, one is obliged to do it. But I did not think that my father would give me so little time to get a job. Finding a job is never easy, and moreover, at that time the country was going through its worst economic crisis in twenty years. Not only were few people being hired, but most companies were also firing their oldest and most expensive employees and not hiring anybody.

So, here I was, a newly graduated computer science engineer, with the need to start working to maintain myself in less than a month or I was going to be in big trouble without my father's allowance.

I started looking for a job. Day after day I looked with no results at all. There were few opportunities for a young man with little experience. The part-time jobs I had worked when I was a student were not much help in this regard. And the country was in one of the worst economic crises in its history. So it was going to be more than an odyssey to get a job in the time my father was giving me.

Fortunately, in less than a week, I had a great first interview with a multinational computer company, the second most important such company in the world. Then I had an incredible number of interviews with several human resources executives and some of the technical wizards in the company. I was tested for everything from how I thought to how I dressed, and I had to pass a physical exam. Hallelujah! They decided that I was the one they wanted to work with, and they hired me as a software specialist. Now I could sleep without worrying that the end of the month was coming up and I might have no money to eat and pay my bills.

Finally—and I am sure a lot of you have had this same feeling—I could tell my father thanks for all he had done for me, and from now on I could fly by myself, and he did not have to tell me anymore what to do or how to do it. At the time, that was my most important thought, even more important than the fact that, in less than a month, I had finished my degree, graduated from one of the most prestigious universities in México, and then gotten a very well-paying job at an amazing company within a week. I would be doing what I really enjoyed, working in the field I had studied for, despite a very convulsed economy that wasn't giving many opportunities to people like me.

So I started my job and kept on seeing my girlfriend, Maru. She was in her last semester of college. She was going to graduate at the end of the year with a degree in economics, and we were already making plans to get married because we did not want to be separated. We knew that if she did not find a job in Monterrey upon finishing her degree, her mother would make her go back to live in her hometown, and we did not want that, as the economic crisis had not finished yet and jobs were still difficult to find.

We planned everything we needed to do to get engaged exactly as the traditions of our country demanded. My father accompanied me to see Maru's mother, where we asked for her daughter's hand in marriage and made our engagement official. We decided to have our wedding in the first month of the following year, just after her graduation, so that we could live together and be able to keep our love flowing.

Seven months passed by. Sometimes the time went fast and sometimes slow, depending on the matter at hand. When I was doing routine things, it went fast; but when we were planning the wedding, it went slow. We had to look for the wedding dress, plan the reception, arrange for the church and everything related to the wedding mass itself, choose invitations, and make the list of guests we wanted to invite. Of course, my mother voiced her objections about anything she disliked, and then came an argument, et cetera, etcetera; but the time went by implacably. Fortunately for my intense desire to be with her for the rest of my life, the wedding day finally arrived.

CHAPTER TWO

THE PROBLEMS BEGIN

Finally, here I was at the church with Maru by my side for the ceremony to be husband and wife forever, because our love was so strong that it was to live on even after death, not just for our life in this world.

We made our wedding promises in front of God and went off as happy newlyweds to live together and be happy forever after. Or so we thought.

Once married, we decided to start a family right away. There was no reason to wait; our country's economic problems were still not resolved, so my wife could not get a job, but I was earning very good money, so there was nothing stopping us from completing our love with a child.

Then my wife was pregnant, and we waited, with all the love we had for each other and huge expectations for what our son could bring to our marriage: love, happiness, and all those little moments with laughter and tears, everything children bring to the lives of their parents. One year after our wedding day, we were at the hospital where my wife would deliver our first child.

The problems started as soon as my wife got to the hospital. The doctor told us that the boy was showing signs of fetal distress, so she had to have a caesarean immediately to avoid more complications for our son. So, he ordered the surgery at once, and then we went into the operating room together, because the doctor accepted my wish to be there with her. All our senses were altered because we did not know what was going to happen to our child and, of course, to my wife, who was having this major surgery.

There we were in the operating room. I wore a blue robe from my toes to my neck and a mask on my face so I wouldn't transmit any infections to my wife or the baby. Everything was sparkling clean and sterilized. Huge bright lights shone down from above her. She was on the operating table, her vital signs being monitored by all the electrical devices doctors use, whatever they are called; of course, the technical jargon is completely absurd and annoying for us normal people. Then they came, the team of nurses in their white uniforms, and started taking care of all the medical instruments. After them came the anesthetist, who put some strange liquid in my beloved wife to get her to sleep and then applied a mask to her mouth and nose for the last part of the anesthesia process. Finally, the doctor came, looking like an alien in his operating gown, ready to open up my wife and, for the two of us, save our child from all the illness he could have.

Before I go on, let me tell you about the chief nurse. She was an old, grumpy lady with a voice like a barking dog, and she looked exactly like one of those dogs with angry faces that seem to be against everybody they look at. This chief nurse did not want me to go into the operating room to be present for the surgery because, some minutes before, they had done another caesarean where the husband, a huge man, had fainted as soon as the doctor started to cut his wife open. Unfortunately, when this man fainted, he fell against his wife, causing a lot of problems and making an easy operation a very complicated one. So the chief nurse did not want me to be the cause of another incident like the one she had just been through.

The doctor issued his order with a very calm voice, the one that people who know they are the boss use to establish their authority and make all those below them do what they want them to do. "He will enter the operating room with his wife."

The nurse replied in a pleading voice, "But, Doctor, what if he faints just like the other one? He is also a big man; he could make the same mess the last one did."

"That will not happen, right, Sergio?" said the doctor, asking me for my compliance. Without waiting for my response, he continued: "And if you can't help it, promise me that you will fall anywhere except on her. All right?" Then the doctor put on his gloves and went to the operating table without the slightest hesitation, because he was not expecting me to answer; he simply assumed that I agreed.

So, there I was in the operating room with my wife as she lay sleeping from the anesthesia, and the doctor started to open her up to get our child out of her womb. When I saw the blood beginning to flow from the open cuts, I started to feel dizzy, my head started to spin, and I was sure I was going to throw up and fall forward. But, with great effort, I pulled myself together. I reminded myself that she was the one who was suffering, not me, and that I really wanted to see my son's birth.

Besides—or maybe mainly—I did not want to give the head nurse the satisfaction of being right about me. I was determined not to let her win in the doctor–nurse situation.

So I stayed put, the doctor kept on operating, and, finally, he took out our baby. At exactly the moment Sergito came out of my wife, he started to scream loudly, as if telling everybody that he did not want to be slapped by anybody—at least, that was the doctor's comment. But as I looked at my newborn baby's face, with his eyes open so wide, I was sure he was crying out of happiness that he finally was out of that small space and in the world.

OUR SON! OUR FIRST CHILD HAD BEEN BORN! But the joy was not complete or permanent. He looked as if something was wrong with him. You could tell immediately from the way his little body was rolled into itself and from the color of his skin. Still, to my wife and I, he was the most beautiful boy on Earth. Or so my wife thought. I agreed with her so she would not be upset with me. I could not disappoint her at that precise moment, when she had just gotten out of surgery and was in a lot of pain; but my son—and this will be our secret, please do not tell anybody—I thought he looked like a beautiful little monkey. Have you seen a little monkey with big eyes and its body curled up tightly, afraid of the whole world and holding onto its mother for theirlife? They are very cute, but I never told my wife that I thought our son looked like a monkey. So, she is going to find out when she reads this book.

My wife, now a new mom, went to a hospital room, and our baby went into an incubator. And we waited for the moment the doctor would tell us we could go home with our child and go on with our lives.

One day went by. Our son was starting to seem a little bit better, and my wife was eager to have him in her arms and take him home. On the afternoon of the second day, a nurse came and told us that the baby wasn't ready to leave, so we had to stay at least one more day at the hospital.

I went running to see my son. He was in the incubator, now twenty-four hours older than when I had last seen him. He had changed from a little defenseless just-born baby to a stubborn, strong, determined just-born baby, fighting with all his just-one-day-old resources. He was completely determined, from the moment he got out of his mother's shelter, to survive and thrive in this world.

And yet he looked so weak, so amazingly fragile as he fought for his life. He was a very small boy, less than five pounds at birth, so you can imagine how hard it was to see him in that incubator and not to be able to hug him, kiss him, and protect him and, mainly, make him feel that his parents loved him with all their hearts and really wanted him to stay alive and be with them no matter what.

"What is the problem with my son, Doctor?" I asked him as soon as I saw him approaching my wife's room. "Is he going to be okay?"

The doctor spoke gently but firmly, as if he wanted me to be very clear on what was happening. "Your son had a lot of fetal distress, and he even swallowed some amniotic fluid. Because of these problems, he is regurgitating his food. His weight is also very low. So, we must keep an eye on him to see how he is coming along."

I was desperate for more information. "But is he going to be okay? Are we going to be able to take him home with us?"

"Not yet," the doctor told me. "We have to wait and see how he does over the next twenty-four hours before I can give you any prognosis. For now, he must stay here in the incubator." Then the doctor entered my wife's room and proceeded to examine her to find out how she was doing.

Feeling very sad, I went inside, trying to hide my mood so as not to burden my already suffering spouse. I went right to her side to watch the doctor examine her. Then he said the words we had been expecting and at the same time fearing to hear: "She can go home." So, we were really happy that she, the strong woman that she was, could go home and resume normal life, but we were really sad that our little boy had to stay at the hospital.

We started preparing to take our things home. Of course we knew we would come back to be near our son; my wife would not think of leaving him at the hospital alone. I went to make the arrangements for my wife to be discharged and for my son to be well cared for in the newborn's pavilion. It took us some hours to fill out all the paperwork.

When we were ready to leave, the head nurse came in, her face grumpy as usual (although we had gotten accustomed to it), and she said (not very happily, I thought): "The doctor says your son is doing much better now, and you can take him home with you. He thinks you can take better care of him at home than anybody here at the hospital can." But I could tell this nurse had more to say, as if it would kill her from the inside if she didn't: "Not that I agree with him. I am convinced that he should stay here; you are not going to be able to give him the care we have here. But he is the doctor, so . . ." She trailed off without finishing that last sentence.

We went numb. Wow, we can take our precious son with us? YEAH, let us do it!

My wife could not wait for the nurses to bring Sergito to us, so we went to the newborn's pavilion to get him, even though she was in such great pain she could barely walk. She was determined to take him into her arms, grab him, and surround him with her love. Finally, we got him in her arms. His little baby face was filled with joy because he could feel our unconditional love. We headed for the hospital door, ready to go home and begin our life together.

The doctor was waiting for us at the door. His final words to us were: "He is sick, so take good care of him. Expect the unexpected. He is going to have some big problems in the future. Good luck, and congratulations."

We thanked the doctor for everything he had done, and we went home to start life together with our new child.

Three days later, we had to rush him back to the hospital. He was almost dying because of the regurgitation and other serious problems. We took him to the emergency room, and immediately they gave him a plasma transfusion to strengthen him so he would not die.

Because he had so many problems and looked so sick, the hospital called a geneticist to examine him. Her diagnosis was: "Your son has a mortal syndrome. He has at most **three months** to live. Not more!" She told us directly with no regret nor any kindness, without even thinking about our feelings as parents.

We were devastated. Here we were with our first child, with all our expectations and love for him, and our hopes for a great future had been destroyed. So what we were to do? Just wait for our son to die?

We sat in the waiting room for days, waiting to see what was going to happen to him, expecting the entire time that they would call us in to tell us that our child had died. But, at the same time, with each day that passed, our faith grew stronger that he was going to make it. And we were going to be there to support him, to fight together with him to get him out of all his problems so he could make it through life as best as he could and with the help of God.

After another terrible three days, they released him from the hospital with an unbelievably bad prognosis: he was expected to live just another two and half months and no more.

But, in our hearts and our minds, this was not an obstacle, it was just another road to be traveled. So we wrapped our arms around him, took him home, coped with our life, and proceeded to live our unexpected journey and enjoy the time we would have together and the privilege of being with our son.

So the journey began, and for the next twenty-one years—yes, you read that correctly, the next twenty-one years, not just three months as they said—we were in and out of the hospital with Sergito. Most of these times, he almost died. But thanks to the **four words**, we not only survived these difficult times, but we were also very happy, and we made our life outstanding despite all the troubles and bad times. These four words—which I will tell you about soon—just came naturally to us. We found them early in this incredible journey and put them into action without knowing it. Later on, in talking with my wife, we defined them and kept on practicing them.

Right now, my son is thirty years old, and my daughter, who was born with the same mortal syndrome, is twenty-five, and they are doing okay. Of course, they have problems and situations because of their syndrome. For example, their physical size and intellectual and emotional development are comparable to those of a ten-year-old child. But they are okay, and we are doing just fine and we are a very happy family.

CHAPTER THREE

FINDING THE FOUR WORDS

"**H**ere comes the doctor." My wife's voice brought me back to reality, to the hospital where our son was being operated on because he could not swallow anything, not even his own saliva. We had been waiting more than five hours for the results of the operation.

My wife said, "The surgeon looks exhausted, but it appears that he finally finished destroying the hot dog Sergito tried to eat."

"Yes," I said. "Let's go ask him."

I could not continue talking, because the doctor came straight to us and started to tell us about the results of the operation and how Sergito was doing:

"It was a very difficult operation. As I told you before, he tried to swallow an entire hot dog, and it got stuck at the end of his esophagus and blocked it completely."

Then the doctor gave us a very full explanation of everything that happened during the five-plus hours of surgery.

"At first, we could not get even a little opening because of the softness of the food he ate. As soon as we got a little hole, we had to proceed very slowly. If we had pushed even a little too hard, we could have broken through his esophagus, and he would have bled to death, just like if he had an ulcer."

The surgeon kept on describing everything that he had done with a watchmaker's precision. "So, it took us almost an hour to make that first opening and another four hours to clean up everything, finishing with a complete check of his digestive system to make sure everything is fine. So, he is okay now, but of course he is completely sedated from the huge amount of anesthetic. He will have to stay tonight at the hospital. When he wakes up and we see that his condition is good, then you can take him home tomorrow."

As the doctor finished telling us his very formal summary of all the things that happened, I thought I saw a faint smile on his otherwise very serious face.

My wife and I looked at each other, then asked the dreadful question that was on our minds. "But he is okay now? Is he going to be able to eat as before? Or is his esophagus badly damaged? Please tell us the truth; we want to know what to expect when he wakes up."

Hearing that Sergito could have died on the operating table—something we have heard many times now—took my mind back twenty-nine years to the very first time Sergito needed surgery on his esophagus because of his mortal syndrome.

When he was just seven days old, he was discharged from the hospital for the second time in his very short life. We went back to our normal way of living: I went to work every day, my wife kept house, and our little son did what babies do: sleep, eat, cry, et cetera.

The days started to pass completely normally, with no problems, until he was three weeks old, when we had to take him in for another surgery. But that is another story. For now, I will just say that time went by, and when the fearful deadline of three months arrived—remember, the geneticist had given him just three months to live—my son was doing well. In fact, even with all the problems he had, we could say he was having a normal life.

You can imagine that when he passed the three-month mark, we were ecstatic because we thought, "If that date has passed and he is still alive with us and very healthy, or at least not as sick as he could be, then that means he is not going to die, he is going to survive and live with us forever." That thought was on our minds all the time, and it was all that mattered to us at that moment.

And then the four-month mark arrived. The only thing in this world that never stops is time. It ticked along very slowly, letting us be happy with our new hope that our son was staying with us, that he was not going to leave us.

Four months after Sergito's birth, I had to travel to México City. We decided to take a little time off our problems and daily struggles and go together, the whole family, to the nation's capital. We arranged things so that when I was done with my workday, we could go out to eat together, go shopping, or at least be together most of the time.

So we went to México City, very happy to be together, spending three days just for us, forgetting the problems we all have in this life. On Friday, I did my work at the office, and at night we went out to dinner. The next day, Saturday, I also worked, and we went out to eat after work. That night, my wife and I had a wonderful evening, with no worries about our son's life or his health.

But, at the end of this truly short three-day mini vacation, it happened!

Sunday came, the resting day of the week. We got up a little bit later than we are accustomed, went out to eat breakfast, and came back to the house we were staying at, with my wife's family, to watch the final game of the Mexican soccer league. My son was sleeping in his crib on the second floor, and I was downstairs watching the soccer game on TV. My wife and her sister went out to buy something for lunch. Suddenly I started to feel worried. My heart felt very heavy, and my thoughts went immediately to my son. Even though he was sleeping upstairs, and I was downstairs, I sensed that something was very wrong with him.

What I just told you happened in my mind in about two nanoseconds. I got up immediately and went upstairs to Sergito, and this is what I found:

He was lying face down, not breathing at all. When I took him in my arms, he felt like a rag doll with barely any weight at all. His eyelids, fingers, and toes were completely violet, the way a hematoma looks after a very hard blow. I could not feel any pulse, so I tried CPR to get him back, but it did not work.

I started crying, yelling, and screaming at the top of my lungs, asking God why He had to take our son and saying every harsh thing that passed through my mind. I had almost lost my mind from the pain when thankfully my wife and her sister came into the room, having heard all the commotion. When they saw the situation, my wife's sister took the baby from my arms and rushed him to the nearest hospital to get him attended.

The doctors said that he was not dead, that he had bronchial aspiration, which means that some fluid, instead of going to the stomach, takes the wrong route and enters the lungs, causing suffocation. The doctor said they got him back from that state, but, as I described to you before, I am completely sure that he had been dead and that he went all the way up to heaven in front of God and said to him:

"God, I know you want me to come sit here by your side, but I am sorry to tell you that I have two parents down there who are suffering a lot. They really love me and care for me; besides, I really want to live and do many things for them, my family, and the world. So, please, send me back to the world to continue with my life."

And I believe God decided that that little boy was right in what he was saying and sent him back to Earth—not to enjoy life, at least not at that very moment, because he had to be admitted to the hospital for four months, but to be a lesson to all the people in this world who are searching for hope and a way to turn adversity to opportunity.

Well, after coming back to life, he had to stay for almost a week in the emergency room. For the first three days, he could not even breathe by himself, so he had to be connected to a ventilator until he could breathe alone. After recovering his breathing capacity, Sergito stayed in the ER for three more days, unconscious. The doctors were not sure he would be able to wake up and react normally again after his episode of bronchial aspiration (I keep wanting to say after his death). We did not know how long he had gone without oxygen, so no one could guess how severely his brain might be affected.

Miraculously, after one week he woke up and started to recover his health. But the doctors had to do a lot of tests, because nobody knew why this had happened to him. We needed to know how to prevent a recurrence if possible, or how to prepare in case it happened again. Therefore, Sergito stayed at the hospital for four solid months. This was not without consequences. During this period, he was put through countless tests, and he was already weak due to his serious syndrome, so he started coming down with illnesses that are in the air at any kind of hospital, but even more so in a public hospital.

We had not thought about whether to take him to a public hospital or a private one. When I found my son dead and my wife and my sister-in-law jumped into action, we took him to the closest hospital. We just wanted to get him back alive; we did not care what kind of hospital it was. But as time went on and we saw that emergencies such as this one were going to be a regular occurrence in our lives, my wife and I decided to keep taking Sergito to public hospitals. There were two very important reasons for this decision:

First, even though no one wants to think about the cost of treatment when a very close relative is sick, it is something one must be very aware of. If an illness is lengthy, the family can end up with no money at all, and then they cannot keep on providing healthcare to their loved one, and that is not going to help get him or her cured.

Second, doctors at public hospitals are normally highly experienced. Every day they provide surgeries and care to severely ill patients, so they go through these things not just once but many, many times. They are very capable of coping with any condition and getting patients well, even more so than private doctors. In fact, many times private doctors go to public hospitals to keep their skills up to date so they can remain at the top of their specialty.

Therefore, most of Sergito's many hospital admissions have been to public hospitals. When it was not possible to go to a public hospital, of course we took him to private ones.

After Sergito had been in the hospital for four months, the doctors finally found out the reason for the bronchial aspiration. He had a hiatal hernia. This was the cause of the severe regurgitation that he had been experiencing since he was born, and all of this was a direct consequence of his syndrome.

But, as I told you before, because of the significant amount of time my son had to be in the hospital, and because of his weakness, he got several more infections. These led to very big problems that several times put him on the brink of death. We hated the nights when we had to sleep in the general admittance room with no possibility of seeing our son, constantly expecting that the voice coming from the speakers would call us by his name to tell us that he had died.

But, as it had started, so it ended. The director of the hospital decided to discharge my son from the hospital even though he had a severe urinary tract infection and a 106-degree fever. He said he preferred that we take care of the infection and fever at home, because otherwise Sergito would keep going from illness to illness and might never leave the hospital. As we took our son to the house where we were staying, we talked about all the problems he had had during those several months at the hospital, and we agreed that whenever you have to stay in a public place with so many people who are having problems, you will see that there is always somebody with bigger problems and more difficult circumstances than yours.

So, we brought our very sick son to the house where we were staying, hoping that he would get well. He had a very bad fever. It seemed that every time Sergito got out of any hospital, he was extremely sick, and yet he fought with all his strength and survived, thanks to his amazing will to live regardless of his limitations. We passed through another two weeks of very hard times in México City, but at the end, he got a little bit better and we were able to go back to our real home in Monterrey and once again resume our normal life.

Fortunately, the next two or three months were calm. Sergito did not have any big problems other than the usual things one encounters with a very new baby who has a very unidentified syndrome. Having not so much to worry about in those months, my wife and I were able to spend some hours relaxing and thinking about everything that had happened during the last ten months of our lives. We really took these conversations seriously. In addition to putting our finances in order, arranging medicines and therapies, and learning more about everything that had happened, we started talking about ways we could share everything we had learned to help other families in similar situations.

"Hey, pay attention to what the doctor is telling us." I heard the voice of my wife and felt her elbow in my ribs, so I came back from my memories to listen to the doctor.

"What are you thinking about?" asked my wife. "Don't you think it is enough that Sergito is sick, and we must learn about everything that happened in that operating room? Do not daydream; concentrate on the here and now."

The doctor finally answered our question about whether Sergito would be able to eat normally. "He is okay now. Of course, he is very highly sedated, so it will take him another three or four hours to wake up. His esophagus is traumatized because of all the time the endoscope had to be in him as we destroyed the hot dog. Therefore, he may not be able to swallow easily for a few days, but it is nothing more than what I just told you. With time it will get better, and he will be back to eating as he did before."

Then he added with a soft but firm voice: "Oh, by the way! Please be very careful that he does not eat a whole hot dog again or anything like that, because the next time we might not be able to get it out. Better keep him away from those soft foods."

My wife and I looked at each other, and at the same time we started to tell the doctor, "We are very careful about what our son eats." We explained that it was hard to keep him away from bad foods because sometimes he would find the things he liked and go hide someplace to eat them, even if he wasn't supposed to. We said we would try to be even more careful about it.

Waiting in the hospital room where Sergito lay recovering, my wife and I started to talk about everything that had happened during the first few years of our son's life. Moreover, five years after Sergio was born, we had a baby girl, Maru, with the same syndrome, and her medical issues, while not as severe as Sergio's, were similar. From those difficult times, we had learned something about the way to respond to adversity. We did not just survive; we changed the obstacles and bad moments in our life into moments of love and joy. The tough times had given us reasons to be closer to each other and to grow as people. Because of the hardships, we had learned to approach marriage, parenting, and family in a more conscious way than we would have otherwise.

Despite all the difficulties, we were happy. Not only that, our view of the present and the near future was optimistic and bright. How was all this possible?

We had talked about these things before—during those few months of peace and calm after Sergio's four-month hospitalization, when he had seemed to be dying continuously due to one infection after another, and before the next hospitalization.

My wife and I realized that our remarkable happiness could be explained by four words that, when you really take them seriously and practice them every day, can change everything and make your life and those of everyone around you much better. I believe these four words can change obstacles and problems into opportunities and new paradigms for others, too. They can lead you into happiness and success, if that is what you want, or at least help you exchange hurt and suffering for calm, peace, and acceptance—because there is much more than just this life and its problems.

And those four words we had been practicing—at first without knowing it, and later with real intention to put them into action every day and every moment—are:

1. LOVE
2. COMMUNICATION
3. HUMOR
4. FAITH

If you love yourself completely, if you love your family, your coworkers, and everybody that surrounds you . . . if you know how to communicate, really communicate, with all of those . . . if you enjoy your life and find things to laugh about in all its aspects, even the problems . . . and if you have faith that everything is going to be okay and accept with joy and hope what the universe thinks is better for you even as you fight with all your strength to get what you think is better for you . . . then you will make it, you will have a better life, you will have loving and caring people surround you, and, most important, you are going to be really happy.

In the next few chapters, I will show you examples of my family and other families putting the four words into action. I hope the examples will convince you of the truth of what I am saying, and I hope that you will see ways you can apply these words to your life to get the happiness and the results you desire—for yourself and for the ones you love.

If you need something in particular pertaining to one of the four words, you can go ahead to that specific chapter, because each of the following chapters is independent of the others. You can also look for a specific word in the stories and read the parts of the stories where that word is applied. I think, though, that the best way to do it is to read the whole thing to be able to implement all four words. Whichever way you think is best for you, just do it, and you will see the results immediately.

CHAPTER FOUR

DOCTOR FOR A NIGHT

"**D**octor! Doctor!" A nurse had come running to where I was sitting, and she was screaming at the top of her lungs and pulling my arm to wake me up.

"What's going on?" I asked in a sleepy voice, trying to shake myself out of a very restless sleep.

"Doctor, Doctor," the nurse kept saying, "Jandra is bleeding to death. We need you to come to help her."

"What?" I whispered. "What do you mean, 'come and help her'?" I could not understand why she was asking me to help.

"Yes, Doctor, Jandra is bleeding to death. You should come to help her and try to stop the bleeding. What do you want us to do?" continued the nurse. She was waiting for me to give orders to help Jandra. I sensed from the look in her eyes that the nurse was also desperate for me to take the pressure and responsibility off her in this precarious situation.

Finally, I was completely awake, but still, nothing made sense to me. I kept looking inside my head for answers to these questions:

Why is this nurse calling me Doctor? I am not a doctor; I am just the father of one of the seriously ill patients in the hospital.

Actually, my son's hospital bed was right next to the bed where this girl Jandra lay.

Why is this nurse expecting me to take charge of what was happening in that hospital ward?

And lastly—this question was for me—what was I supposed to do in this situation?

One month earlier, we had brought two-year-old Sergio to the hospital yet again because his esophagus had closed completely. Acid reflux caused by his syndrome had burnt it, and he could not swallow anything, not even his own saliva, so he needed surgery to open it and let him eat again.

So, he had the surgery. He had some complications, some of them very bad and others very easy to solve, which meant another month in the hospital. That was the beginning of the path that led to this problem I was now having. Because our son was not dying, nobody was allowed to stay with him at night. I do not know why the doctors thought it was unnecessary for seriously ill patients to have someone with them at night. When your loved one is in a really serious state, even if they are not dying, you still want to be with them.

Anyway, despite this policy, my wife and I still wanted to be with our son twenty-four hours a day whenever possible. We were not concerned with our own fatigue after more than a month of waiting outside the ICU while Sergio recovered from the surgery. We did not care if we had to sleep in a chair in front of his bed or outside in the hall. We did not care whether we ate or not. We did not care at all about our comfort; we only cared about being with our son so we could watch him get better and help him, if we could, with anything that he needed.

Because of the many times our son had already been in this hospital, most of the staff recognized me and my wife. But not all the nurses and doctors knew that we were not doctors. They would see us looking thoroughly through his medical chart—which we understood well, having heard the medical terms and expressions so many times—and they would assume we were doctors. As a result, we weren't asked to leave at night, and this became the solution to our problem. But let me clarify, we never told anyone that we were doctors. We just didn't correct them when they called me Doctor. And a lot if not most of the hospital staff did.

So here I was at three in the morning of this particular day, sitting on the couch in front of the first-floor hospital ward. I had been watching my son from that position because there were no chairs inside the ward, it being a general ward. Due to the hour, I had fallen asleep, exhausted from all the time spent at the hospital and the various stressful situations concerning our son's health. And this was when the nurse came running towards me, screaming:

"Doctor, Doctor, Jandra is bleeding to death. We need you to come to help her."

My first impulse, once I was completely awake, was to run away and never look back, because I wasn't a doctor at all, and I was not going to be able to do anything to help this young girl.

Jandra, a girl who couldn't have been older than thirteen, was sick with an acquired immune deficiency syndrome. But it was not the kind of AIDS we have all heard of, the kind caused by the virus called HIV. Rather, she was sick because in her poor, actually really poor home, her mother used pesticide to keep all the bugs, roaches, and rats at bay. Because Jandra kept inhaling this pesticide, she lost her immune system, which is precisely what AIDS is.

This girl, just thirteen years old, was dying, bleeding to death in the last hours or minutes of her existence, and you could see the fear in her beautiful olive eyes, because she was alone and she knew she was dying and nobody could do anything to help her.

Her little body, consumed by her illness, was skinny. You could see the bones of her arms and hands through her grey skin. Her legs were wrapped in layers of clothing, as her skin could no longer keep her warm. You could tell she had been a beautiful girl when she was healthy. Her almond eyes with their amazing olive color still had some sparkle in them whenever she had something to laugh or at least smile about.

Her hair had mostly fallen out, leaving only a few lifeless locks, and her cheekbones were prominent because there was little or no muscle left in that scared, girlish, dying face.

After looking for just a second into those still beautiful eyes, I could see that they were asking me to be with her and give her some comfort so that at least she would not die alone. Without hesitation, I screamed back to the nurse: "I am a therapist doctor; I do not know how to help her with medicine or what she needs." I said it because I did not want to lose the privilege of staying with my son at night, but at the same time, I had to let this nurse know that she had to get a real doctor to help Jandra.

"I will stay with her to comfort her and try to stop the bleeding. Meanwhile, you get the doctor to attend her." I finished with an order: "Get the doctor! Now! GO!"

I turned away from the nurse without waiting for an answer from her, and I walked to Jandra's bedside. I took her hand in both of my hands and stroked her fingers gently to calm her, and I talked very gently to her with loving and comforting words, all while looking into her eyes, which were amazingly sad and full of tears.

"Jandra," I said, "I am here with you. Our Lord is with you, and you are going to be happy with him for all eternity."

She said, "But I am going to die and will never again be able to see my mom and my little brothers." She was crying now.

"Do not worry for them," I said. "You are going to be by God's side, so you will be a guardian angel for them, and you will take care of them directly with Our Lord."

Her thin face was right in front of me, and I could see her fear starting to fade slowly, because she was feeling the love that I felt for her, and I kept on telling her everything I could to comfort her and make her feel loved.

Suddenly a doctor came and abruptly ordered me, without any kind of consideration: "Move away from her. She has AIDS, and you could get infected from her touch if her blood contacts any opening in your skin."

Immediately, Jandra looked fearful and tried to withdraw her hand from mine. I kept her hand firmly in mine and said, "Do not worry, little child. Nothing is going to happen to me. I love you, and God will be with the two of us now, because you are an angel, and soon you will be with Him to look after me, too!"

The doctor and the nurse looked at me as if I was completely crazy. They just looked at me and then at each other and back at me again, unable to understand what I was saying. Then they turned their attention to trying to stop Jandra's bleeding.

But the girl understood what I said. She understood that true, unconditional love for another human being is possible with no remorse or hesitation, and in that moment, I also understood that love, when transformed into action, is one of the most powerful words we have for making our world a better place.

The nurse's voice brought me back from my thoughts: "You can let her hand go now, Doctor; she is dead. Nothing more can be done for her. She died calmly, and it seems that you minimized her suffering." Then the nurse turned and walked away to attend to the necessary paperwork.

I looked again at Jandra's young face. She looked calm; her features were relaxed. You could see that, at the end, she had felt the true love that I wanted her to absorb. She had understood that she was going to be an angel and that she would always have the love that her mother and her brothers felt for her even though they could no longer express it the way they had in the past, and she knew she would be keeping an eye on all of them from her seat in heaven beside Our Lord.

I felt really sad and devastated because a very young girl had just died, but at the same time, I felt grateful to God for giving me the opportunity to give this girl a little peace and a lot of love at the very end of her existence, filling her last moments with love and comfort so that she could die in peace, feeling loved and not alone.

For me this was a very important experience. I learned that if you love yourself enough to do what you think is right, even in the hardest moments of your life, you will be able to give love to your fellow man and get love back in the process, and, in so doing, you will take some huge steps toward making this world a better world for all.

THE FIRST WORD:

LOVE

Love is the first of the four words that, when put into action, enabled my wife, my two children, and I to live perfect lives, even after the worst predictions about my children's chances of survival. **(Remember, the doctor gave Checo no more than three months to live.)**

CHAPTER FIVE

A GRANDMOTHER'S MISUNDERSTANDING

For almost two hours, the old lady had been crying. She was sitting by the side of a baby who was lying sick in the bed right beside Sergito's. My little boy was sleeping—or, I should say, trying to sleep.

It was three in the morning, yet all the lights in the general ward of the public hospital were on, as they always are in public hospitals. I had never understood how in the world the doctors thought patients could sleep with bright lights on. Between the lights and the old lady's crying, I had gotten no more than twenty minutes of continuous sleep. The same was true for most of the interns in the general ward.

Sergito had been lying in that bed for almost a month, recovering from one of the many surgeries he had already undergone in his young life. He was seven years old, well past the life expectancy doctors had predicted when he was born.

For the first two weeks after this latest surgery, Sergito had been in the ICU, almost dying, surrounded by the mechanical and electrical apparatus that was keeping him alive. Thank God, he had an incredible will to live. Finally, he was moved to the general ward to recover. Now he had been there for almost a month, watching a lot of the other patients arrive, get better, and leave. Fortunately, he was getting stronger and healing well. It was a very slow process and very painful, but at least he was getting better, and we had the hope that he was going to live and get out of the hospital sometime in the near future.

Therefore, hearing this lady crying and weeping the whole night, making it impossible for anyone else to get some badly needed sleep, you can imagine how it made me feel.

I thought to myself: *I do not know why she is crying so much.* Somehow the baby was sleeping peacefully despite the lady's crying, and he did not seem to be seriously ill. Besides, he was in a general ward where the patients were supposed to be getting better. But I did not know anything about his circumstances, so maybe my assumptions were completely wrong.

I decided to walk over to where the lady was crying and ask her why she was so inconsolable and, maybe, give her some support just by talking to her and listening to her concerns.

I stood up from my chair, walked over to her side, and asked her, "Are you his caretaker?"

"No," she answered, turning her weeping face to me. Her eyes were already red and swollen because of how long she had been crying. "He is my grandson."

"Is he very sick? What is the problem with him? Why do you cry so?" I wanted to understand what was happening with this little baby. He was still sleeping and breathing peacefully, despite his grandmother's weeping—unlike most of the others in the ward, who were wide awake and listening to my conversation with the woman.

She took a little time to sneeze into her handkerchief. After drying her eyes, she looked at me and answered: "He has pneumonia. He has been very sick, and he could not breathe." She started to weep again. Sobbing, she finished: "He had to be brought here this morning."

"All right," I said with my kindest and most understanding smile. "But the doctors have seen him and given him the medicine that he needs, is that so?"

"Yes, of course, but my poor baby, he is so sick." And the woman started to cry even louder than before.

I smiled very kindly and compassionately. "Come on," I said, "he is going to get well. The doctors have already seen him and given him the medicine that he needs. Pneumonia is almost 100 percent curable today, so you do not have to cry for him." This grandma clearly loved her grandson, so much so that she felt terrible about his having a disease that is widely known to be curable, unlike some of the others in the ward who had more serious diseases, some of them even deadly.

But here she was, crying incessantly, and her grandson was starting to get restless hearing her.

"But he had heart surgery and has been really sick," she managed to tell me in between her sobs.

That hit me really hard in my feelings, because there is a huge difference between somebody who has pneumonia that can be cured with antibiotics and someone who has it following a heart surgery, which is a major operation with many potential complications during recovery. I thought about how inconsiderate I had been, and I resolved to change my way of talking to this grandma.

I asked her, "And how is he doing? How long ago was the surgery done?"

She stopped crying for a moment. After blowing her nose and cleaning her face with her handkerchief, she answered me: "He had heart surgery when he was one and a half months old."

"And how old is he now?" I asked her.

"Almost three," she said.

I wish I could tell you that I reacted calmly when she told me her grandson's age. I wish I could tell you I had gentle thoughts, such as how wonderful it was that he was completely cured now, or how great it was that God had given him and his family the opportunity to have him alive and well for nearly three years. But that would be a lie. I felt angry. So, I went back to my seat.

At exactly that moment, the baby woke up, looked at his grandma, and, seeing her completely covered with tears, started to cry also and could not be stopped.

Immediately, the grandmother stopped crying and reached to the baby with amazing love and tenderness, took him in her arms, and started to console him by singing a lullaby. In less than fifteen minutes, he was asleep again.

The woman put him back into his bed, moving slowly and taking care not to wake him up again. Then she sat beside him in the same chair that she had been in the whole night. She bent towards her grandson, rested her chin on the bed's handrail, and started to cry again.

I got up instantly from my chair and walked back over to the old lady. I really wish I could tell you that I was kind and patient with her, but no! I was really mad that this grandma did not understand what had just happened. I was mad that she kept on doing the wrong thing for herself, her grandson, and all the other patients in the ward.

"You had better stop crying," I said with a harsh voice and more anger than I had wanted to express.

"What?" she said. She seemed annoyed at what I had said rather than understanding why I had said it. She kept trying to say, "My grandson here is sick, and I . . ."

I stepped right in front of her and did not let her continue. "Stop that nonsense," I snapped. Then I withdrew my anger and tried to make her understand her mistake. "I know your grandson is sick, and I do understand how you feel, but don't you think that everybody in this room has a really close relative who is sick, and that they also feel heartbroken and distressed because their relatives are here instead of enjoying life outside?"

She just looked at me.

I continued, "All of us are sad, some more than others, depending on how sick their loved one is. We all want to cry, but you can see that most of us are not doing so. On the contrary, we try to laugh and make this horrible time for our children the best it can be. I understand that your grandchild had heart surgery, which I'm sure was a huge problem, but that was almost three years ago. By now he is completely healed from that operation and happily recovered from it. So, you should forget about it, as your grandson has already done."

"But I . . ." she protested.

I raised my hand. "No," I said, "do not say anything. Just listen to what I am trying to tell you here. Your grandson is fighting to get well from pneumonia, but he thinks that he is failing because every time he sees you, you are crying. Your crying makes him think he isn't going to get well."

"But I didn't mean that . . ." she tried to explain.

I finished my speech. "So, you should laugh instead, telling him happy stories so he can see you happy, and then he will understand that everything is going to be okay. That will make him get well sooner than seeing you sad and crying. Do you understand what I am saying? Remember, he is the one who is sick and fighting and suffering, not you." She looked at me with a serious expression on her face. For the first time that whole night, she was completely calm and not crying. She said to me: "I am sorry. I understand now that my behavior was not the best thing for my grandson. I was just letting my feelings out, but the communication I was giving to him was wrong. I misunderstood what I was telling him with my tears. I thought he could feel that I was sad because he was sick, but what you have just told me made me understand. Thank you for that, son." A small smile appeared on her otherwise sad face. Then she got serious again. "But you should not have told me with that tone of voice, young man. Remember that I am older than you, and you have to respect me."

I hung my head down, gave her my apology, and went back to my seat to watch my son sleep.

In the end, she was right. I should not have raised my voice. But she did understand what I wanted to tell her, and everybody else in the ward was able to sleep a little that night.

THE SECOND WORD:

COMMUNICATION

Communication is the second of the four words that enabled my family and me to navigate the challenges posed by my child's severe syndrome and lead fulfilling lives despite the doctors' predictions of a limited lifespan for him. **(Remember, the doctors gave him no more than three months to live.)**

CHAPTER SIX

LAUGHING AT THE EDGE

Jose's laugh resounded through the entire first floor of the public hospital.

He started to yell with all the force of his little lungs, "Here comes Bello Pongo! Here comes Bello Pongo, I can hear him bustling around!"

In México, all people receive two last names. The first one is the father's last name, and the second is the mother's last name. So my son's full name was Sergio Bello Pombo, but in Jose's childish speech, Pombo was "Pongo." So he kept yelling to everyone, whether they wanted to hear him or not: "Here comes Bello Pongo, here comes Bello Pongo, I can hear him bustling around!"

And it was true: Sergito (the diminutive form of Sergio) and I had just walked into the hospital. My son's syndrome caused regurgitation, and the stomach acid had burned his esophagus. On this day we had an appointment to have his esophagus checked to find out if it was healing well or if surgery would be required.

Jose was, at that time, a little child no more than six years old. My son and I had met him at the hospital during one of his many stays due to his multiple illnesses. We had come to love

Jose for his joyful love of life in spite of all the pain and trouble he had experienced with his family.

He came from a wrecked family. His father, an alcoholic, used to beat up his mother all the time until he died because of the alcohol. Then Jose's grandfather took over the dad's place as the authority in the family, and the grandfather's approach was more angry than loving, and, sadly, he started to beat the mother and Jose as well.

His mother did not do anything to stop the beatings or to defend Jose from his grandfather, so this kept going for a long time, until one day, unfortunately for Jose, Granddad came home completely drunk when Jose was alone and sleeping in his bed. Their house, if you can call it that, was a cardboard box no more than four square meters in which the whole family—the mother, three children, and the grandfather—had to live. So here came the grandfather, drunk and completely out of his mind, noisily knocking down everything in his path. When he reached Jose's sleeping body, he started to beat him and undress him. Jose fought back with all the strength he had in his little body, hitting him, scratching him, and crying out for help, but this small house was at the end of the poorest quarter of the city, and nobody listened, or, more likely, nobody wanted to get involved in this kind of situation. So, finally, with a very strong blow to the head, the grandfather knocked Jose unconscious, and then he finished undressing him and raped him.

From then on, every time this man came home, usually completely drunk, he abused Jose and made him do things that he did not want to do, and Jose had to comply, fearing that he would be severely beaten if he did not do everything his grandfather asked him to do.

Jose begged his mother to help him, but she did not believe him at first. Then one day she came home early and found the grandfather doing all those nasty things. But instead of stopping him and throwing him out of the house, she just turned around and let him do all those things, time after time.

Jose was an amazingly joyful child in spite of all these troubles. He enjoyed all the good things he had, and he was happy with life when he was not being molested. And he never thought his mother was an accomplice of his grandfather; on the contrary, he showed her all the love and affection he felt for her.

So, on this day, when my son Sergio finally entered the hospital room, Jose ran to hug him and yelled, "How are you, Bello Pongo? I missed you all this time, my friend!"—shouting so everybody in the hospital could hear him.

My son could not talk, so he just hugged Jose in a very tender way, showing all the love he felt for him.

"Mama, Mama," Jose shouted, "Sergio just hugged me! He loves me, he loves me!" Then Jose went running, jumping and laughing through the halls of the hospital.

All the doctors, patients, and families who knew Jose's story were completely astonished by his love of life and the enjoyment he took in everything, even after all the problems he'd had to overcome.

Because of the beatings and the abuse that his grandfather had inflicted on his little body, Jose was losing his sight. Finally the doctors sued the grandfather to force the authorities to bring him to justice or at least order him to stay away from Jose.

At this moment of his life, losing his sight and having all these big problems with his grandfather, Jose was an incredible example of how to enjoy life, showing all the good things we can enjoy despite everything that troubles us.

"Mama, Mama," shouted Jose, "can I play with Bello Pongo? Can I? Can I?"

"Yes, Jose, of course you can play with Sergio," replied his mother, laughing with delight at how happy he was to be able to play with Sergito. "But be careful. You know he cannot play with you the same way other children can. He is a special child and has some problems with his movements, so you have to be very gentle with him."

I watched Jose and my son very closely when they started to play together. Jose was very kind with Sergio, acting as the big brother but laughing all the time and really enjoying the chance to play with somebody he could take care of instead of being taken care of himself.

After they had played together for several hours, Sergito and I had to leave the hospital. We were really sad because we did not know if we would see Jose again and enjoy his laughter and joy for life.

Some months later, we were back at the hospital for Sergio's usual checkup, and we hoped we might see Jose again. We were expecting to hear his yelling and laughter when we got to the hospital, but there was no commotion at all. I asked the doctor what had happened to Jose, and he told me the bad news that Jose had died.

One night, despite the restraining order that had been in place for several months, his grandfather came to the house and found Jose alone. Jose's mother had gone to work. The grandfather came into the house and beat Jose until, finally, God took the child to his glory and let him rest from all this pain and horror.

When I think of Jose, I always smile, remembering his childish face, his laughter at everything he found amusing, and the joy he put in everything he did in his life. He never resented the trials God sent him, and he really enjoyed being alive despite all his suffering.

For me, this is a very important lesson. I learned that even if you have problems, it is still possible to enjoy the good things in your life and appreciate the people who love you. If you put humor in your life and enjoy life as it is in spite of your problems, you might even find a way to solve those problems. At the very least, you will be happier, and life will be more enjoyable.

I can still hear the happiness in Jose's voice as he laughs and screams with all the force of his lungs, "Here comes Bello Pongo, here comes Bello Pongo, I can hear him bustling around!"

THE THIRD WORD:

HUMOR

Humor is the third of the four words that, when my family and I put them all into action, enabled us to surpass the problems associated with our two children's mortal syndrome and have the time of our lives, making the most of the very good lives Our Lord gave us the privilege to enjoy. **(Remember, the doctor gave Checo no more than three months to live.)**

CHAPTER SEVEN

GOING BACK HOME

It had taken the surgeon more than five hours to break up and remove the hot dog our son Sergio had swallowed whole in his yearning to "eat like the rest of the world does." At the end of the afternoon of the next day, at last we got to take Checo home from the hospital. His entire esophagus hurt from the endoscope, but we were happy that everything had gone well. "Finally, we are going home, Chequito, my little darling," said my wife to our son with such an amazing loving voice that Sergio just looked at her and started to doze in her lap.

"We must take much more care with Sergio and his meals, especially when he goes to other places outside our house," I commented.

"Yes," said my wife. "We have to be sure that when we are not with him, he has someone to take good care of him, someone to watch what he does and not let him eat something he shouldn't, as he did this time." She said this with a sly look on her face, as if she were an accomplice of this little kid.

And so we did find somebody to look after Sergio all the time. There were no other adverse events for some time, which gave me the space I needed to remember some of the things Chequito had to overcome in order to survive.

As I have mentioned, the reason he had so much trouble with his esophagus—actually, part of his esophagus and some of his colon—was severe burns from stomach acid due to regurgitation caused by his genetic syndrome.

When he was born, we were told he would live for only three months. Yet he kept on living. As time went by, he had to go to several hospitals due to his syndrome. Most of those times, everybody expected that he would not survive.

As I'm sure you remember, when he was only four months old, I found him dead in his crib and we had to rush him to the children's hospital for revival and urgent attention. Following that crisis, he had to be hospitalized for four months. Next, he had a recurring problem in which his throat would close completely, making him unable to swallow anything, even his own saliva. Sometimes this even made it difficult for him to breathe. Each time this happened, the doctors had to operate to open his esophagus.

Finally, his doctor at the children's hospital—the doctor who attended him for more than twenty years—said, "He deserves to eat well." He explained to us that Sergito's esophagus was so scarred from all the burns and surgeries that the next time it closed, it might be impossible to open it up again.

"He really deserves to eat well and enjoy his meals," the doctor said again. "It is time to do an operation to reconstruct his esophagus so he can eat normally, or almost normally." This doctor had a very strange way of being serious and almost unpleasant with parents yet really loving with his patients.

"Besides," the doctor continued, "a time is fast approaching when I will not be here, and who knows who else could perform an emergency reconstruction? So it is better that you decide to do it now, while I am here and there is time to do it with calm and preparation." Thus concluded his very long speech to us as

Sergio's parents, urging us to decide quickly about a frightening surgery that was necessary for our child to live a better life.

After the doctor finished talking, my wife and I looked at each other, and I said to the doctor, "Can you give us some time to make a decision?"

He answered, "Okay, but just two weeks, no more." And with that, he ended the conversation and left the waiting room.

We sat there with all sorts of thoughts going in and out of our minds, wanting to make the best decision for our child, but fearing he would not make it through the operation—which, by the way, the doctor had told us Sergito had only about a 5 percent chance of surviving.

So we went back to our house and to the normal life we had with our son. We tried not to think about the conversation with the doctor, as if by doing that we could delay the final decision. But time went by, as time inexorably does, and suddenly the two weeks he had given us to decide were over and we still had to make this very difficult and painful decision.

Finally we made an appointment to take Checo back to the doctor and accept the surgery. Still, we hoped that everything would get better and no surgery would be needed after all.

So, we went to the appointment with Checo, and the doctor said, "Okay, so we will proceed with the surgery. Here is the hospital admittance order for you to sign. Let's get him immediately admitted to the room and prepare him for surgery tomorrow morning."

My wife and I looked at each other and said, almost in unison: "Right now, Doctor? Can it wait until the beginning of next week?"

The doctor answered in his usual rough way: "No, no way. If I give you more time to think about it, you are going to change your minds, and it is very important that we proceed with the operation right now. This is the best time, because it is not an emergency yet and we can plan as carefully as possible."

So, as he recommended, we did hospitalize Sergio in the public hospital to be operated on the next day if possible.

The doctor told us that Sergio's operation would start very early in the morning, and he had to fast for at least twelve hours, so he could not eat anything at all after his early supper, about six in the evening. But his mother, as all mothers are, was concerned that her poor little baby might not sleep well if his stomach was empty, and she wanted him to get to the surgery happy. Moreover, she was not sure if he was going to get out of the surgery at all. So she decided to give him a delicious black bean and noodle soup, which was one of Sergito's preferred dishes, at about eight or nine o'clock that night. Imagine this! Fortunately, he did not experience any vomiting, which is the complication fasting is intended to prevent.

And the time came, inexorably, as is always the case, for the very difficult and dangerous surgery. The nurses took our little boy, Sergio, to the surgery room to make the colon transposition, or so we thought.

But, at the last moment, the doctor decided to change the plan. Instead of doing a colon transposition, he cut away the burned part of the esophagus, moved the stomach up, and reconnected it to the good part of the esophagus.

That description of the surgical plan makes the surgery sound easy and doable in a relatively short time, but this was not the case. The intervention took almost ten hours, which was completely dreadful for my wife and me because we did not know what was happening and nobody came to update us on how it was going, not even a word. So, our thoughts wavered continuously from "Everything is all right; it is just a very difficult operation" to "Something must be wrong and they're trying to fix it" and back again, over and over. The waiting was really, really hard.

After those tremendous ten hours of vacillating between those two thoughts, not knowing which was right and which was wrong, finally we saw the doctor come out. He was smiling faintly, and he told us, speaking very carefully and softly: "We did everything that we could; I think he will be okay, but we will have to wait seventy-two hours to be sure. He will be in intensive care for observation. He has two catheters in his abdomen in order to drain blood, pus, or any other liquid that needs to be expelled from his body after this kind of operation."

So, Sergito was taken to intensive care, and we stayed by his side as much of the day as the hospital would allow. When we could not be with him, we waited outside the unit, taking turns to go eat or take a very fast shower.

And the time went tremendously slowly, second by second, minute by minute, the minutes turning into hours and, finally, the hours converting into days, until the doctor came back to us Friday morning with a sparkling look in his eyes and said:

"Sergio is doing okay. Today we are going to take out the two catheters, because nothing is draining, which means that everything is well inside his abdomen. We will take them out in three or four hours. You should go get some rest and come back then. Go ahead, go and sleep a little." With that, he turned his back to us and left the waiting room.

So my wife and I decided to go back to the apartment, rest a little, and get back in time for the removal of the catheters. But, as we were staying all the way on the other side of México City, it took us about an hour and a half to get to the apartment. As soon as we did, one of our neighbors told us we needed to get back to the hospital urgently.

We called the hospital immediately, and they told us to come back right away because something had happened to our son and his operation.

So we got a cab and got back to the hospital. The doctor was waiting for us, already changed into his surgical scrubs. He just told us, "Everything went wrong; the operation has to be reversed, because something happened and his body rejected the whole operation. We have to put him back as he was before the last operation. We need your permission to proceed."

So, as scared as we were, of course we agreed, and thus started another ten dreadful hours of waiting as they restored Checo's stomach and everything else inside him.

Of course, not everything could be restored, because his esophagus had already been cut and there was no way they could put back that little burned piece they had removed during the last operation.

This operation, as I already told you, lasted more than ten hours. But then the doctor came out to the waiting room and, with a very slight, almost imperceptible smile, told us: "The surgery went almost perfectly. Sergio came through the operation very well, but he is in shock, so you should talk to him all the time in order to ease his awakening from the anesthesia." The doctor went on, looking very proud and happy about what he had done: "His esophagus can't be connected to his stomach yet because of the little piece we already cut off. So he has a small bowel ostomy, and you will have to feed him through that. Also, the secretions that normally go from the nose and mouth down through the esophagus to the stomach have to go somewhere, so the upper part of his esophagus is connected to a temporary stoma in his neck, and there is a bag there which you will have to clean. So, go ahead, good luck, and later, when he gets his strength back, we will operate again to reconstruct his esophagus and connect it to the stomach." The doctor finished his speech, then turned around and left.

We did not get a chance to ask any questions at all, so we just looked at each other, thankful that our son was still alive after that big operation. We were happy, and our hopes started to grow that we would see our son well again.

So, we went to see Checo and talk to him. He looked so little and fragile with all the tubes connected to him, so we felt very distressed, and it broke our hearts to see him in that position.

But, as we had always done, we kept on praying and living our lives. We stayed with him as much of the day as we were allowed to, applying the three words I have told you about so far in this book—love, communication, and humor—but mostly, with all our souls, minds, feelings and hearts, we applied the fourth word, the one we knew would give us the healing of our beloved little son: **FAITH**.

A week later, Checo was moved from an emergency therapy room to a general room, because he was responding perfectly to the treatment and the doctor was hoping to discharge him from the hospital in less than a month.

And so, finally, the time came when Sergio was given permission to leave the hospital and go back to our house and to our everyday life. Life actually was not exactly as it had been before these two surgeries, because we had to feed Checo through his ostomy and clean his neck bag every two or three days, but we had him back with us, and nothing else mattered. It showed that having faith, real faith, really works, as well as the first three words I have been telling you about.

THE FOURTH WORD:

FAITH

Faith is the fourth and last but not the least of the four words. Faith works, and not only religious faith but universal faith, being able to really feel unconditional faith with no restrictions, believing that what Our Lord and the Universe decide regarding our biggest problems is best for the lives of every one of us. It works, because the four of us—my wife, my son Sergio, my daughter and myself—with all the people who surround us, together with a real faith, were able to surpass all the problems related to my two children´s unidentified syndrome and live very good lives. **(Remember, the doctor gave Checo no more than three months to live.)**

CHAPTER EIGHT

DESPITE EVERYTHING, FAITH WORKS!

C heco is still alive and enjoying it.

The doctor said, "He deserves to enjoy his life without restrictions; he deserves to be with his family, sitting at the same table and eating whatever he wants, with no fears about what will happen to him, instead of his family having to hide from him when they eat."

The doctor was standing in his office at the hospital and talking to us about the surgery that Sergio now needed in order to be able to eat normally. Just several months prior, he had endured two very difficult and dangerous operations trying to fix his burned esophagus, and the surgeries did not work as was planned, so he had his esophagus connected to his neck and was being fed through an ostomy.

"So," the doctor continued, "you must decide very soon about the next surgery, while I am still here, because it won't be long before I leave."

"What do you mean by that?" I asked. "Are you going to retire or leave the hospital?"

"No, but I am already old and tired, so I do not know how much time I have left. Therefore, you do not have too much time to decide, and Sergio has the right to eat well."

"Okay," we said, "we understand that. But what are the chances he will survive this colon transposition surgery and get good results?"

We asked that because several doctors had already commented to us that our son could live perfectly well being fed through the ostomy, and we were not sure if it was a good idea to risk his life yet again, now that he had already increased his weight by almost five pounds and looked fine and seemed to be having no problems.

"The chances he will come through safely are at most 10 percent," answered the doctor calmly, looking very serious.

The decision was so important to the life of our beloved son that we could not give the doctor an answer at that moment. "Give us some time to think about it, please, and we will tell you."

"Okay," he answered, "but do not take too much time. As I already told you, time is going fast, and I may not be here much longer."

We left the doctor's office with a lot on our minds, but, surely, no decision at all at that exact moment.

We tried to spend as much time with our son as possible, pretending that nothing was wrong with him, that everything was already fine and that Checo was a very happy child and that we had an amazing and beautiful life with him with no problems at all. And he was doing fine, except that every time we had to eat, we had to hide from him so he would not feel left out. Sometimes he would try to eat normally, but it was not possible, so he felt sad, and sometimes he did not want to eat at all.

However, we did not want to make that very hard decision

that would put his life in grave danger. So we closed our eyes and let time pass by, pretending that he was happy and that we two were also.

Finally, to celebrate my birthday, we had a family reunion, and we went to a restaurant to eat. Most of us have had similar birthday celebrations: having fun, enjoying the food, and, of course, celebrating the birthday. But—and this was a huge but—Sergito was not happy. He was not enjoying anything at all. On the contrary, he was so sad that sometimes in the middle of the dinner he went to a corner of the restaurant and sat alone, sadly watching us as we ate and drank.

At that very moment, my wife and I talked to each other.

"Do you see Chequito?" my wife asked me.

"Yes, of course."

"He looks incredibly sad. He does not want to share our celebration. He feels bad."

"Yes, I can see him. I guess this is the answer to the question of surgery. We cannot postpone it any longer."

"I agree," said my wife. "I am really scared, but if our son will be sad whenever we eat, of course our decision must be what is best for his life and his happiness."

So, we went to México City and told the doctor that we had decided to go ahead with our son's surgery and that he could plan a date to perform it.

He asked his nurse to give us the pass to hospitalize our son to operate on him the next day.

"How come, Doctor?" I said.

"We are going to hospitalize him immediately," the doctor replied, "in order not to lose any more time."

"Yes, we understand," said my wife, "but we did not think it would be scheduled so soon. We thought it would take some time to plan the operation before you finally do it."

"No," replied the doctor, "not at all. I think the best thing for all of you is to do it without delay so we can have Sergio eating as soon as possible. So let's continue with all the requirements for his immediate hospitalization. Tomorrow, or the day after tomorrow at the latest, we can carry out the surgical intervention."

"Doctor," I said in a noticeably quiet voice, "Doctor, would it be possible to wait one more week so we can take him on a vacation trip?"

"I would rather you didn't, because you are going to change your mind and decide not to come back. I think is better to do it right away now that you have decided to proceed."

"We swear, Doctor," replied my wife, "we will come back in one week. Just let us enjoy him for seven more days. Let us take him on vacation to a place he has always wanted to go." We understood that there was a remarkably high chance that this would be our last time with him, and we wanted to enjoy him to the maximum.

Finally, after several more minutes of very intense thinking and discussion, the doctor relented.

We departed the hospital with our little son to take one more week and go on a holiday trip with him. We took that vacation, and it really looked like a farewell trip, even though my wife and I were trying to pretend that everything was okay and that there was not, in the near future, an event that would most probably take away our son's life.

We went on that trip, and then, one week later, we came back to the hospital for that dreadful operation. We did not want it, but, at the same time, we felt our son had to live happily with no restrictions on his eating. So we decided to proceed and leave everything in our God's hands.

Finally the day arrived. They took Sergito to the operating room and started the hours-long surgery to replace his esophagus, already cut during a previous failed attempt, with a piece of his colon.

We waited and prayed. We waited and prayed.

We were completely in God's hands, completely sure that He was going to do whatever was best for our son and ourselves. We had a very solid faith that, whatever the operation's result, it would be the best decision for the happiness of our son.

But we waited and prayed. And we waited and prayed.

And . . .

Finally . . .

The doctor came out from the operating room.

"We did everything humanly possible. Now it is in the hands of God. The operation went well, but your son is in shock, so you must talk to him continuously so he can wake up from that shock."

We were ecstatic when we heard those words. Of course, we did not know at that time what it meant to be in shock. We only cared about our son being alive and out of that very dangerous operation.

"Of course, Doctor," we said, "we will talk to him all the time and stay with him in the intensive care unit every minute we can."

And the doctor left the hospital, leaving us with incredibly happy news but also with a great deal of worry about our child's chances of recovery.

We went to see Sergito in the ICU as soon as they let us in. The first time was really shocking—not because he was in shock, for it looked as if he were sleeping, but because it was almost impossible to find him amid all the electrical instruments that were keeping him breathing, draining fluids, and monitoring his vital signs. So our hearts were really scared, but, at the same time, we were completely sure that God had made a miracle and that our son was going to live and recover completely from this huge operation.

We stayed with him as long as they would let us that day, talking to him and praying. We had the faith that he was going to recover. And then the next day, we went again and kept talking to him, and praying, and we thought soon he would be out of the hospital and we would go back to our lives.

After two days in the ICU with us talking to our son all the time, Checo woke up, and the miracle started to be seen. He was awake, and, really, he was incredibly happy in spite of being in the ICU and still being very weak.

After Checo had been in the ICU for just one week, some of the other patients acquired chicken pox, and the doctor decided to transfer Chequito to a general room in the hospital so he would not get infected. He stayed there for another two weeks.

Finally the big day came. After so many prayers, petitions to God, and an amazing amount of faith, we learned the doctor was finally discharging our beloved son, Sergito, and we took him home to an almost normal life, in which he could eat freely almost anything he wanted and live with us, thanking God for everything that we got back from our prayers and our faith.

AND WE WENT BACK TO OUR LIVES AND STARTED DOWN ANOTHER ROAD THAT LED TO SEVERAL EVENTS, SOME OF THEM PROBLEMATIC AND SOME HAPPY, BUT THAT IS ANOTHER STORY.

Gallery

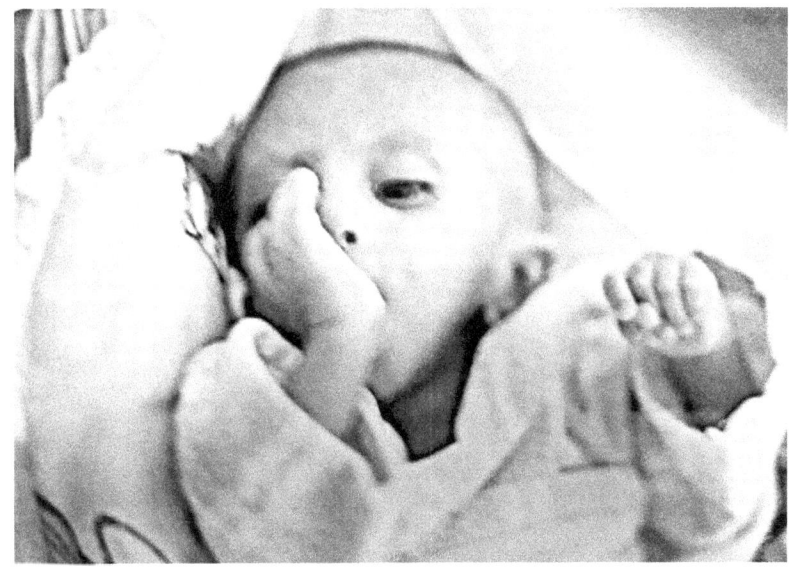

Very sick 4-month-old Checo sleeping in the hospital.

3-year-old Checo at his father's office.

The whole family: Checo, his father,
his sister Marucita, and his mother Maru.

Checo at the beach, just after his esophagus operation.

Checo with his mother and sister.

Checo cleaning his shoes,
feeling so proud of his appearance.

Sergio in the countryside.

Checo with one of his dogs. Checo loves dogs.

The whole family at Checo and Maru's party.

Checo writing.
He loves to work and write all the time.

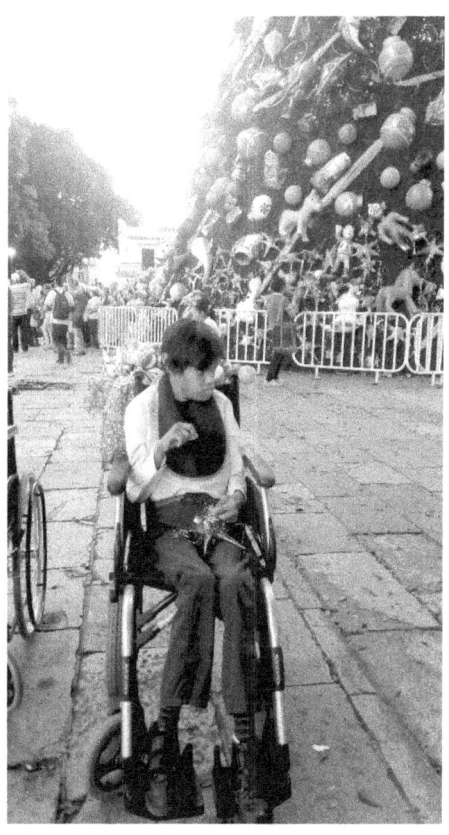

Sergio at the Zócalo of Oaxaca during Christmas.

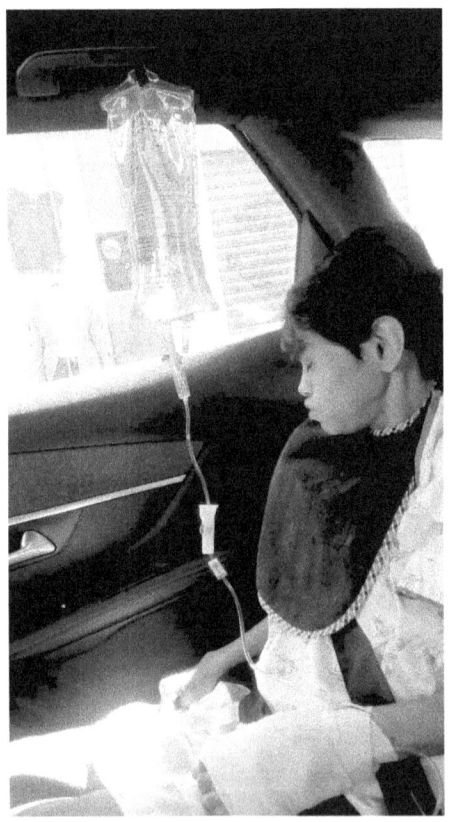

Checo leaving the hospital.

Checo sleeping in a hammock.

About the Author

Sergio Andrés Bello Guerra is a father of two children with physical and intellectual disabilities. Along with his wife, he has gained a deep understanding of the care and attention required for individuals with disabilities. This personal experience has been a driving force in his life, leading him to become a tireless advocate for the rights and potential of all individuals, regardless of their circumstances.

Originally from Oaxaca, this prominent Mexican politician, academic, and writer has dedicated his life to promoting the economic and social development of his state and country. As an engineer in computer systems with degrees from the Monterrey Institute of Technology and Higher Education, Sergio has complemented his education with advanced studies in economic development, legislation, and writing. He has earned various master's degrees and doctorates, including a doctorate in political science and a master's in creative writing, as well as multiple honorary doctorates. His academic career has made him an influential figure in both politics and society.

In the political arena, Bello Guerra has served as a local representative in Oaxaca, notably as the president of the Commission for Economic, Industrial, Commercial, and Artisanal Development during the 62nd legislature of the State Congress.

During his term, he promoted policies aimed at strengthening the local economy, with a particular focus on supporting indigenous artisans and producers. His commitment has ensured that Oaxaca's cultural traditions and small economies receive the necessary attention to thrive, always grounded in transparency and accountability. He has also served as Councilor for Tourism and Transparency in the municipality of Oaxaca de Juárez.

As a writer, Sergio Andrés has published numerous articles and blogs on politics, society, tourism, culture, motivation, and economics. He focuses on preserving Oaxaca's cultural identity and promoting sustainable development strategies. His reflective and committed style highlights his vision of equitable and sustainable growth for all. Through his writings, he emphasizes the importance of closing the gap between theory and practice, stressing the need for effective and realistic legislative work that enables people to recognize and tap into their inner potential.

His written work, both in books and on his blog, serves as a source of inspiration for those seeking to understand the challenges and opportunities we face, approached from a perspective that balances respect for traditions with the need for modern and just growth. Sergio Andrés Bello Guerra is a fervent advocate of the integral development of all human beings, convinced that each individual possesses a unique potential that deserves to be discovered and cultivated.

In recognition of his work, he has received numerous honors in both the political and academic spheres. His constant defense of everyone's rights and his commitment to strengthening the social fabric have earned him the respect of his peers and the communities he represents. With a clear vision and a passion for social progress, Sergio Andrés Bello Guerra remains a key figure in Oaxacan politics and an authentic promoter of human potential in its fullest expression.

www.ingramcontent.com/pod-product-compliance
Lightning Source LLC
Chambersburg PA
CBHW070804120626
46557CB00002B/713